Hudson Bay

QUÉBEC

A

D

A

Montreal

Ottawa

VER.

NEW HAMPSHIRE

NEW BRUNSWICK

Saint John

OTA

WISCONSIN

MICHIGAN

NEW YORK

MASS.

CONN.

Boston

RHODE ISLAND

Atlantic Ocean

IOWA

Grand Rapids

Milwaukee

Chicago

Toledo

OHIO

PENNSYLVANIA

New York

NEW JERSEY

DELAWARE

MARYLAND

Des Moines

A

Indianapolis

Cincinatti

WEST VIRGINIA

Va.

MISSOURI

Louisville

St. Louis

KENTUCKY

TENNESSEE

Nashville

NORTH CAROLINA

ARKANSAS

Memphis

ALABAMA

Atlanta

SOUTH CAROLINA

Little Rock

MISSISSIPI

Birmingham

GEORGIA

LOUISIANA

Jackson

Jacksonville

as

New Orleans

FLORIDA

Gulf of Mexico

Miami

Zone 1 below −50°	Zone 3 −35° to −20°	Zone 5 −10° to −5°	Zone 7 5° to 10°	Zone 9 20° to 30°
Zone 2 −50° to −35°	Zone 4 −20° to −10°	Zone 6 −5° to 5°	Zone 8 10° to 20°	Zone 10 30° to 40°

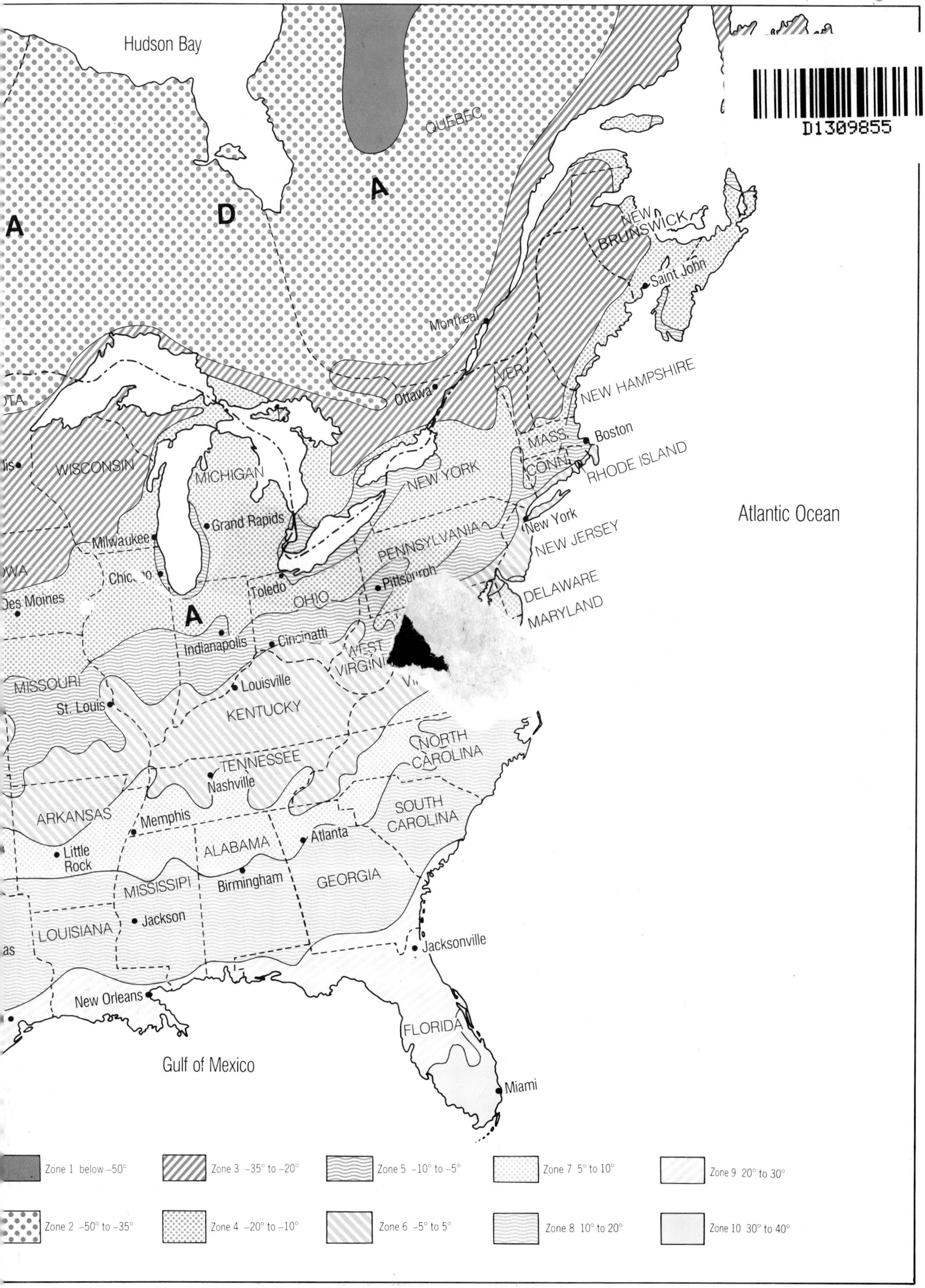

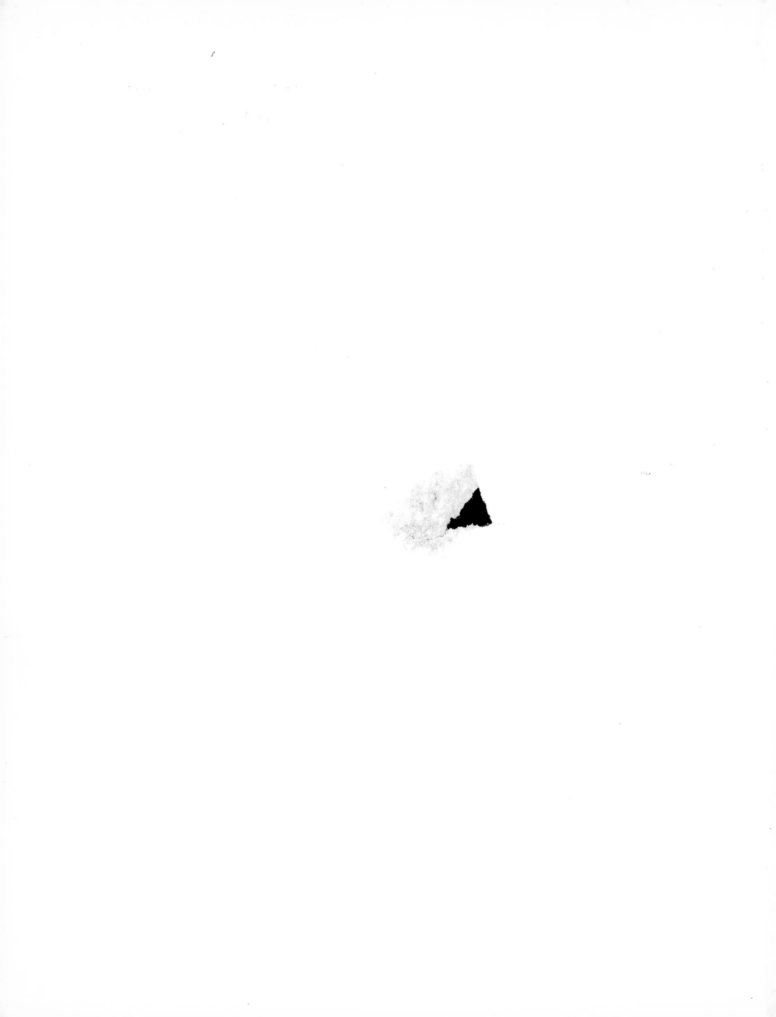

SERIES EDITOR · VINCENT PAGE

MODERN GARDEN ROSES

Peter Harkness

Photographs by Vincent Page

The Globe Pequot Press

Chester, Connecticut 06412

First American edition published in 1988 by The
Globe Pequot Press, Chester, Connecticut 06412.

Library of Congress Cataloging-in-Publication Data

Harkness, Peter.
Modern garden roses.

(Classic garden plants)
Bibliography: p.
Includes index.
1. Roses.   2. Rose culture.   I. Title.   II. Series.
SB411.H 324   1988   635.9′33372   87-32546
ISBN 0-87106-744-7

Produced by the Justin Knowles Publishing Group,
9 Colleton Crescent, Exeter, Devon, England

Design: Gilvrie Misstear
Illustrations: Vana Haggerty
Zone map courtesy of Swallow Publishing Ltd

Manufactured in the United Kingdom

MODERN GARDEN ROSES

ACKNOWLEDGEMENTS

My thanks are due to many kind friends for advice, ideas and information in connection with this book. I am especially grateful to Peter Haring, who contributed the Foreword, and to Vincent Page, who suggested the basic format and took the photographs. I should also like to thank Mrs Jill Bennell, Mr Dick Balfour and Mr Dick Squires of the Royal National Rose Society; Mrs Nan Cocker and Mr David Welch of Aberdeen; Angela Pawsey of the Rose Growers' Association; Mr Tom Robinson of Guernsey; Mr Jack Harkness and Mr Brian Watson of our family firm; Mr Pat Dickson of Northern Ireland; Mrs Bev Dobson of the United States, Mrs Peggy Nicoll of Bermuda, Mr and Mrs Alan Mason of New Zealand, Mr Ken Langton of Australia, Mrs Sue Hauser of Switzerland and Mr Zhongguo Zheng of China for keeping me up to date with rose developments in those countries; the authors of the books cited on page 142; and the skills and dedication of rose lovers, known and unknown, down the ages, who have made the rose what it is today.

Finally, a word of special thanks to Margaret my wife, for her constructive criticism and encouragement with this book, and love and support always.

Peter Harkness, Spring 1988

WINTER PROTECTION

Hybrid tea roses grown in Zones 8, 9 and 10 have no special winter requirements. However, those grown in Zones 6 and 7 may require protection, and those grown in Zone 5 and colder should definitely be covered. If you live in an area in which the temperature falls below 20°F for any length of time and there is no covering of snow, protect your roses after winter pruning by building up a layer of soil (brought from elsewhere in your garden) to cover them to a depth of approximately 12 inches. Do not remove the cover until the ground is completely thawed.